Nutcracker Suite

P. I. Tchaikowsky
For Piano Solo • Arranged by Wesley Schaum

Foreword

This new edition of the *Nutcracker* includes all eight parts of the famous *Nutcracker Suite*, plus four additional selections from the full length ballet.

Page two has a brief biography and portrait of Tchaikowsky, along with background information and the story of the ballet. The sequence of music in this book is the same as the sequence in the original ballet.

Index

Schaum Publications, Inc.
10235 N. Port Washington Rd. • Mequon, WI 53092
www.schaumpiano.net

The Composer

Peter Ilytch Tchaikowsky (chy-CUFF-skee) is one of Russia's most famous composers. He lived from 1840 to 1893. His works include symphonies, operas, ballets, concertos, piano music, vocal music and chamber music. In May, 1891 he visited the United States and conducted four concerts in New York City. This was part of the dedication of Carnegie Hall, now one of the most prestigious music halls in the United States.

The *Nutcracker* was first performed in St. Petersburg, Russia in 1892. The complete ballet has more than twenty-five musical sections and takes about two hours to perform. The *Nutcracker Suite* is a set of eight excerpts from the ballet that are extremely popular as an orchestral piece.

The Nutcracker is a favorite ballet performed during the Christmas season in many cities across the United States. Performances often have groups of dance students on stage included in the action. The ballet has numerous special effects including snow falling, spectacular magic tricks and a giant expanding Christmas tree. There are many elaborate and colorful costumes, especially in the series of dances performed at the Magic Castle. There is lots of action in the mischievous antics of the children at the house party. The battle between the mice and the toy soldiers has vigorous sword fighting. All of this, along with the charming music, gives this ballet a wide appeal.

The Nutcracker Story

The plot is based on "The Nutcracker and the Mouse King" by E.T.A. Hoffman.
The story is set in Russia in the early 1800's. The **Overture** sets a happy, festive mood for a children's Christmas party. The gala event is held in the formal parlor of a large house in the city of St. Petersburg. The room has elaborate decorations for the holiday including a huge Christmas tree.

This is the home of two children, Clara and her older brother Fritz. Their father and mother have invited several other families and their children to join them at the Christmas party. The **March** is played as some of the guests arrive.

(The story is continued on page 6.)

Overture

March

The Nutcracker Story

(story continued from page 2)

When the guests have assembled, a magician arrives to provide entertainment. He has brought mysterious presents for the children including large mechanical dolls and a wooden *nutcracker* carved to look like a small soldier. Nut shells are cracked by placing them in the mouth of the Nutcracker and squeezing the handles.

The Nutcracker is immediately Clara's favorite toy. When she reluctantly shares it with her brother Fritz, he is purposely reckless with the Nutcracker and throws on the floor. Clara quickly rescues the Nutcracker and lovingly puts it to rest in a doll's bed under the Christmas tree. Fritz and his boy friends tease Clara by making lots of noise with toy instruments.

After the party has ended, Clara begs to take the Nutcracker to her bedroom, but her father refuses. After all are asleep, Clara sneaks back to the parlor to look again at the Nutcracker. She is intrigued by a mysterious light coming from the Nutcracker's bed beneath the Christmas tree. Although she is a little frightened, she snuggles up beside the tree and falls asleep.

As Clara sleeps, she dreams that the Christmas tree grows to become extremely big and all of the toys magically come to life. She witnesses a fight between an army of mice and the toy soldiers, led by the Nutcracker (**Battle Scene**). Clara helps the Nutcracker by hitting the king of the mice with her slipper. This ends the battle and the mice disappear.

The Nutcracker is now transformed into a handsome Prince. He takes Clara to an enchanted forest where snow is gently falling (**Snow Flake Waltz**). The Christmas tree is in the middle of the forest. The toys around the Christmas tree gather to honor Clara and the Prince and escort them to the **Magic Castle** in a kingdom of sweets ruled by the Sugar-Plum Fairy. In the castle, the Prince tells how Clara saved him from the mouse-king.

To celebrate the defeat of the mice, a program of dance performances is planned at the castle:
Arabian Dance – Chinese Dance – Russian Dance
Dance of the Reed Flutes – Waltz of the Flowers

The Sugar-Plum Fairy and the Prince perform in the **Dance of the Sugar Plum Fairy.**
The story concludes with everyone participating in the **Grand Waltz Finale.**

Battle Scene

Snow Flake Waltz

Magic Castle

Arabian Dance

Chinese Dance

Russian Dance

Dance of the Reed Flutes

Waltz of the Flowers

Dance of the Sugar Plum Fairy

Grand Waltz Finale